# Gallivanting Auntie

♥ Teaching you how to live vicariously through

the children in your life!

♥ Doing this without a computer

## by

## Linda Barlogio

**Gallivanting With Me**

Corona, California

# Gallivanting Auntie

Published by
*Gallivanting with Me*
*Corona, California*


Copyright © 2016 *by Linda Barlogio*


Illustrations by Linda Barlogio

ISBN: 978-0-9905747-1-2 (paperback)


Printed in the United States of America

To all aunties everywhere, who want to spend more time with their nieces and nephews. ♥

♥ GALLIVANTING AUNTIE ♥
Corona, California

Dear Reader,

After hearing several aunties share their desire to have a closer relationship with their nieces and nephews, I wrote this book with them in mind, especially those that, for one reason or another, don't get to see the children in their lives often.

My sincere hope is that you will not only enjoy the wacky story, but that you will complete the activity in the back and invite your niece or nephew to play with you by sending them the thin Auntie version of yourself, the passport, and the letter with simple instructions. (Don't worry – I included a sample!)

It's a great way for you to visit their day-to-day life and adventures and begin to interact with them in the activities and topics that are important to them.

I know that you will cultivate happy memories about the places you and your extraordinary kids have visited. It might even be fun to create an Adventure Album for all the pictures they send, especially if you do the activity with more than one niece and nephew.

Happy Gallivanting!

Linda Barlogio

Once upon a time, long ago, in a faraway land called The City of Orange, lived Auntie and Flash, a very large Maine Coon cat who was the love of her life. She lived in this quaint, old-fashioned community in the center of Orange County, California. Auntie has a full life because she not only takes care of Flash, but she also works in the local library's Historic Preservation section. She absolutely loves everything old, especially her 1910 redwood cottage. Her dear friends, Ethel and Lula, who are also aunties, live on either side of her and they often get together for walks in the "Orange Plaza." It's a small park right in the middle of the city that showcases a beautiful fountain in the center.

If you are ever In Orange, especially in The Plaza near the fountain, you might see Auntie walking Flash on a very long rope leash! He likes to be near the fountain because he loves to put his paws in the water and watch the birds as they take a bath in the top of it.

Even though Auntie has a full life, there is something missing – time with her nieces and nephews! She and her friends often discuss the fact that despite having lots of wonderful things to do *and* adorable cats, they don't get to see their nieces and nephews very often.

This discussion is always a hot topic when they go out for lunch at Barbara's Victorian Tea House. "We really almost never get to see these kids! It seems that the grandparents get to have all the fun with them - more than we aunties do! Isn't it important to have <u>ALL</u> family members involved in the raising of children?" Auntie asked her friends. They all nodded in silent agreement.

"Well, if we knew more about technology..." Ethel started and then shook her head. The aunties know that if they understood more about the current technology, such as Facebook and texting, they could communicate that way, but they all think that it just takes up too much of their time! Flying is not an option either, because all of them are on a fixed income and they can't afford the airfare.

Auntie's good friend, Gallivanting Granny, had told her about making a wish and trying to dream up a solution to a similar problem. Granny said that she did this and even though her wish wasn't answered in the way she thought it would be, (who would've thought that she would end up being mailed to her grandkids), It wasn't nearly as traumatic as she anticipated and she has been having a wonderful time with her grandchildren ever since!

However, Auntie is much more practical than that since she is a librarian she uses her intellect and mature wisdom to help *her* make decisions... not wishing on a star! Now it has been several days since she talked to Granny and Auntie has not had a single clever thought about what to do.

One day, Auntie and her colleague, Susanna, were working with the artifacts in the Historic Preservation section when a group of "Red Hat" ladies, (yes, Ethel was a Red Hat Lady) came for a tour. They were very interested in what the section had to offer about the history of Orange County and the City of Orange, in particular. Most of the ladies had family members that helped found the city so the ladies wanted to know everything there was to know!

HISTORIC PRESERVATION

DEPARTMENT

Some of the ladies were a little too
curious! They tried to reach for
the boxes on the top shelf
~ boxes they could hardly even see!
Though they weren't very strong,
the ladies began lifting one
another so they could get to those
tempting boxes that were really
out of reach!
You might guess what happened next!

Oh Noooo!

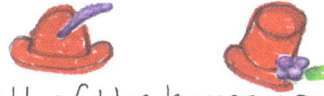

All of the boxes came crashing down right on top of Auntie! Oh, what a catastrophic sight! It was unbelievable! The ladies were so alarmed, they started running in all directions, their red hats flying everywhere!

Susanna tried to lift the boxes off poor Auntie. Jim, the maintenance man, jumped into the kerfuffle and the situation became even more chaotic! But they finally got the boxes off and at the bottom of it all was Auntie ~ a very thin Auntie!

When they got Auntie up, she was so shocked that she stood completely still and could not move! Luckily, Ethel was there. She wrapped her coat around Auntie and slowly led her out of the library. By this time Auntie was coming to her senses and even though she was stunned, she was not visibly hurt - just very thin!

The minute Ethel got Auntie home, she put her to bed with a hot water bottle and some soothing music to help her calm down and go to sleep. Ethel called Lula and they decided to meet the next morning to see how they could help Auntie through this very perplexing situation.

Live
Love·Laugh

The three of them met at Barbara's Victorian Tea House and were served special Orange Blossom Spice tea and some delicious caramel scones. Unfortunately, they really couldn't eat much because they were so distraught. Auntie proposed that they contact Gallivanting Granny and ask for some help. Lula agreed to take care of the task. Ethel said she would contact Granny's friends, Marilyn and Molly, to see if they could help too. Auntie said she was still very upset, so she was going to go home and take a nap and they all agreed to meet at Auntie's house that evening.

By evening Auntie felt much better but she was still *thin*! Ethel reported that Molly and Marilyn were out of town visiting their grandchildren, but Granny was there and she said that since Auntie wanted to have a better relationship with her nieces and nephews, why not mail her to them? Just wrap the very thin Auntie in a small quilt and put her in one of the post office's snazzy boxes like Marj had previously suggested when Granny went on adventures with her grandchildren.

Auntie wanted to stop and think about this because post office trucks can be dark and scary places! Granny reassured her it would be okay; she had been afraid too, but she had a great time! Auntie realized that since Granny had an adventure visiting *her* special kids, she *could* do this too. In fact, the *more* she thought about it, the *more* excited she became! She asked Ethel and Lula if they could go to the post office and get one of those great boxes because she really wanted to get started!

When Ethel and Lula got back from the post office, they called Marj to see if she had a small quilt to line the box. Marj looked in her old trunk for the perfect one and brought it over. It was in Auntie's favorite colors too!

Ethel, Lula, and Marj carefully packed Auntie into the box, tucking the quilt around her. They included a passport for Auntie and a letter she had written to explain how the family members could connect with one another without using a computer. Auntie was so glad that she had talked to Granny because it helped alleviate her apprehension.

Auntie was so amazed that this was actually happening! She was no longer afraid and everything was perfect: the idea, the quilt, the box, and good friends to send her on her way to her dear nieces and nephews!

# Activity

1.  Make your thin Auntie look like you!

    Make her look as much like you as possible: hair color, eye color, glasses, etc. Her clothes can be your favorite: dresses, pants, or even a sweatshirt and blue jeans! You could possibly send along a coat for cold days or a sundress for sunny days. (Magazines can give ideas for dressing your "Auntie".) Use all of the resources you have (crayons, markers, colored pencils, scrapbook paper, etc.) and remember that the children in your life are your audience - not the art critic for the local paper!

2.  Write a letter to your niece or nephew and invite them to play!

    Not sure what to say? Don't fret! I've written up a sample letter on the next page, which includes the instructions. All you need to do is customize some of the words and phrases to make it sound like YOU wrote it!

3.  Send Auntie, your letter, and the passport to your niece and/or nephew!
4.  Let the FUN begin!

# Sample Letter

### Customize it with your own words and phrases.

Dear _____,

     I am sending this letter because I would love to go on adventures with you. You are probably wondering how I can do that since I live in _____ and you are in _____. But, I have recently become acquainted with someone who can help us.

     Her name is Gallivanting Auntie! Can you see the resemblance? She's a super thin version of me! I had to make her thin, so I could send her through the mail.

     I would love it if you would please let her (Me!) accompany you on some of your favorite day to-day activities such as visits to the store, the park, or on any fantastic adventures you might have. I really want to see for myself where you go and what you do!

     How will I see? Good question!

     Well, you'll have to ask your _____ to take a picture of you and Auntie wherever you go. When you have taken your pictures, ask your _____ to print them out so you can put them in this handy-dandy passport I've sent you and then tell me (on the page next to the picture) where you were when you took the photo and what you liked about your adventure there.

     I hope this will be fun for you. I can't wait to see the pictures, with me included, and hear about all of your exciting escapades!


All my love,

# GALLIVANTING AUNTIE PASSPORT

Auntie visited here: _____

With: _____

On: _____

Auntie visited here: _____

With: _____

On: _____

Auntie visited here: _____

With: _____

On: _____

Auntie visited here: _____

With: _____

On: _____

Auntie visited here: _____

With: _____

On: _____

Auntie visited here: —————

With: ——

On: ——

Auntie visited here: —————

With: ——

On: ——

Auntie visited here: _____

With: _____

On: _____

Auntie visited here: _____

With: _____

On: _____

# THE END

Continue the Adventure

Please send pictures and stories about the escapades "you" and your kids have taken if you would like to share them with other aunties. Linda anticipates putting together a book of these wonderful adventures, so we can inspire others to get out there in whatever way they can!

Contact Linda if you would like to surprise your auntie friends with a fun workshop experience where they can have an enjoyable time and learn some easy techniques to improve communication with their nieces and nephews as well as to manage the change that happens when these wonderful children come into our lives!

An easy way to stay connected with Linda is to visit:
www.GallivantingWithMe.com

## Stay tuned for new adventures with Auntie. More books to come!

# About the Author

After working as an adjunct counselor and instructor for more than 14 years, Linda Barlogio recently retired from Chaffey Community College where it was her passion to help students figure out what they wanted to do when they grew up – something she says she is still working on for herself!

As a mother, grandmother, auntie, educator, and counselor, Linda has experienced the reality that communication across the generations is not easy. We all have expectations that are not readily met, and this is where the stressful situations arise. She received her Master's in Education, with a focus on counseling from the University of Redlands and then worked for 18 years with both young and mature adults in the field of Education and realized that communication issues are at the heart of all counseling dilemmas. When she discussed these dilemmas with her friend, Marilyn, who is a psychologist, they realized just how important it was to fill this communication gap with grandparents as well as aunts and uncles too. Thus the idea for this book was born. Linda knew she had to write it and get it to as many grannies and aunties as she could!

By writing *Gallivanting Auntie* and conducting corresponding workshops with aunties in her community, Linda's mission is to give support to aunties in their attempts to play a bigger part in their children's lives.

Linda lives in Corona, California with her husband, Jim, and their dog, Dusty. She has three children, seven grandchildren, one great-grandchild, and numerous nieces and nephews.

# Thank you to…

Aunt Mag, (Margaret Bliss) for giving me a wonderful example of what an aunt should be!

Susanna Branch, for your support and insightful marketing ideas.

Marilyn Rock, for your knowledge, thoughtful inspiration, and friendship.

Marj Grayck, for your courage, support, and love.

Molly Dillon, for your wonderful writing expertise and friendship.

Wendy Whitney, for your delightful first critique that didn't include, "You've lost your mind!"

My husband, Jim, for your quiet patience with the outlandish schemes I often pursue.

Vernette Mackley, for your very long-time friendship and kind, generous support.

Aurora Lavado, for your clarity and insight just when I needed it most!

Barbara's Victorian Tea House in Etiwanda, CA for your scrumptious tea feasts.

All the students at Chaffey College and Corona-Norco Adult Education, for the challenges and struggles that you have overcome. You have helped me find my own courage to take a risk, too, and get out of my comfort zone.

The Red Hat Society for allowing me to use some of their ladies for my book. If you would like to participate in their fun outings, please contact them at redhatsociety.com

And last, but not least, Amanda Johnson and True to Intention. Without you all, this book would still be a "good intention" and we all know what happens with those!

www.ingramcontent.com/pod-product-compliance
Lightning Source LLC
Chambersburg PA
CBHW060854270326
41934CB00002B/135